MOVE OVER, ROVER

MOVE OVER, ROVER

What to Name Your New Pup
When the Ordinary Just Won't Do

KYRA KIRKWOOD

ILLUSTRATIONS BY DAVID SEMPLE

Clarkson Potter/Publishers
New York

Copyright © 2009 by becker&mayer!, LLC

All rights reserved.
Published in the United States by Clarkson Potter/
Publishers, an imprint of the Crown Publishing
Group, a division of Random House, Inc., New York.
www.crownpublishing.com
www.clarksonpotter.com

CLARKSON POTTER is a trademark and POTTER
with colophon is a registered trademark of Random
House, Inc.

Move Over, Rover is produced by becker&mayer!,
LLC, Bellevue, Washington. Authored by Kyra
Kirkwood, and illustrated by David Semple.
www.beckermayer.com

Library of Congress Cataloging-in-Publication Data
Kirkwood, Kyra.
    Move over, Rover / Kyra Kirkwood. — 1st ed.
    1. Dogs—Names.   I. Title.
    SF422.3.K57 2009
    636.7—dc22   2008037108

ISBN 978-0-307-45357-0

Printed in the United States of America

Design by Laura Palese

10 9 8 7 6 5 4 3 2 1

First Edition

TO MY "LOVING, FULL OF GRACE" ANNIE,
AND TO OWEN, MY "YOUNG FIGHTER."
YOU TWO OPENED THE WORLD TO ME,
AND FOR THAT I'M FOREVER GRATEFUL.

CONTENTS

INTRODUCTION

What's in a **NAME?**

To each of us, no other name in the world is more meaningful than our own. Whether we love it or hate it, our name shapes our future and influences our personalities. The process of naming a child often takes the entire nine months of pregnancy. But with a leap of faith, new parents choose a name that feels right, sounds good, brings them joy whenever they hear it, and hopefully fits their child's future looks and personality.

Naming your new puppy can require the same amount of deliberation—with a few key shortcuts.

Picking out a meaningful, elation-inducing moniker is vital, because you're guaranteed to say it dozens of times a day. Unlike with human infants, these fur babies give us a big advantage in the name game: We can use their personalities and temperaments to help guide us to the perfect name, since puppies' personalities (unlike humans') blossom very early on in many cases. Using these clues allows us to discover a name that we'll cherish—and that will fit our newest family member for life.

Welcome to Move Over, Rover, a tool to help you dig through the confusion of locating the perfect name for your pup. Gone are the Spots and Rovers of days past. Welcome home Atticus and Sydney and Chance. Instead of choosing names based on tradition (Fido) or appearance (Fluffy), this book will help you match names to puppies' personalities in an effort to settle on the truly perfect combination.

Sure, as a dog grows, his disposition will evolve along with his physical characteristics. Some hyper, silly pups grow into laid-back, lazy adults, and some timid youngsters become extroverted as they age. But for the most part, you can pick up hints of your canine companion's emotional makeup early on. The personality test on page 13 is a great way to determine what type of pooch you have: a happy-go-lucky one (the Cheerleader), a bossy dog (the Don), a slow-moving sloth (the Couch Potato), a shy pup (the Wallflower), a high-maintenance beauty (the Diva and the Pretty Boy), an athlete (the Jock), a hard worker (the 9-to-5er), or an independent soul (the Lone Ranger).

By connecting personality traits with names, you're sure to find one that not only sounds pleasing, but is original and suitable as well. There's just something off when you see a bossy dog named Sugar or a shy pup answering to Cujo. You want a name that sounds good, feels great, and fits. There's nothing worse than yelling, "Come here, Mr. Von Stinkypants!" to your Akita across the dog park—for you, or him.

After you've tested your pup's personality and determined the best fit, flip to the appropriate chapter to find names suited for this type of dog. There are more than 150 personality-appropriate names and their meanings packed into this little book. Some sound like the disposition they're describing (Fiona for a Diva), while others have meanings that embody the personality to a tee. Who wouldn't equate Lulu, meaning "soothing, comforting," with a Couch Potato?

Each chapter also includes a description of the most common breeds that embody the personality type. Chihuahuas are famous Divas, and it's hard to picture a 9-to-5er without seeing a border collie. But this isn't to say a border collie can't be a Jock, too, or a Chihuahua a Don. All dogs are

individuals, regardless of breed. Don't fear if your Great Dane is a Wallflower, or your Jack Russell a Lone Ranger. Mixed-breed puppies may possess DNA from typical Couch Potatoes (Newfoundlands) and Dons (German shepherds), so who knows where they will end up on the personality spectrum? Use the breed listings as guidelines, and trust your puppy's lead when it comes to deciphering personalities.

Take a peek at the numerous sidebars peppering the book, too. We've included everything from dog-training tips to celebrity pooch names to help make your first few weeks with your new family member as easy and enjoyable as possible.

Remember, *Move Over, Rover* offers general guidelines to help you find a fitting name for your new dog, but it's not to be used as a temperament test or evaluation. For example, while Wallflowers act shy, they are not fearful. Dons are alpha and bossy, but not aggressive. Traits like those need professional evaluation and behavior work; your trainer or veterinarian can recommend a good behaviorist to contact right away.

So sit back, get comfy, and embark on the first of many great adventures you and your dog will have together.

Woof!

PUPPY PERSONALITY TEST

Take some time to get to know your new companion throughout the day. Run around outside; play with the dozens of new toys you purchased; gaze at her sweet, fuzzy face; and be on the giving and receiving end of lots of kisses. Try to figure out what your new pup is all about—she's probably doing the same with you. When you have a moment to yourself, sit down and complete this quiz. Write down the numbers for each question you answered yes to, then compare them to the answer key below the quiz. Whichever category most of your numbers fall into is the one that best relates to your pup. If your dog fits into more than one category, follow your gut and choose the most appropriate personality type for your puppy and breed, or explore names for both personality types. Flip to the corresponding chapter, and find the best name for your new dog.

DOES YOUR PUPPY . . .

1. rush to greet you enthusiastically and frantically, even though you've been gone for only ten minutes?
2. become positively focused on a toy or ball?
3. act stubborn and refuse to listen?
4. enjoy time by himself or herself, alone in another room?

5. shy away from new people and experiences?

6. sleep a lot, especially after a short playdate or walk?

7. love to jump all over the place, all over the furniture, all the time?

8. hate to get messy or dirty?

9. wag his tail all the time, even in his sleep, and every time he meets a new face?

10. seek things out around the house and bring them to you?

11. try to order you around by barking at you?

12. pay you little attention?

13. whine and cry a lot in new situations?

14. act motivated only when food is involved?

15. enjoy nothing more than a long run around the neighborhood?

16. adore being groomed?

17. act full of life, like an innocent two-year-old, no matter what's going on?

18. nip at your heels in an attempt to herd you into an area?

19. tell you when it's time to eat or play?

20. not get involved with playtime and prefer to just sit quietly and ignore the goings-on?

21. shake, quiver, and shiver a lot?

22. love nothing more than a belly scratch, ear rub, and nap on the couch?

23. sacrifice food for a chance to play?

24. require being held quite often and seem insulted if she is on the ground?

IF YOU ANSWERED
"YES" **TO QUESTIONS** . . .

- **1, 9, 17:** Your puppy is the Cheerleader, the ever-happy, always enthusiastic pooch who embodies the stereotypical dog image and loves squeezing every joy out of every minute of life.

- **2, 10, 18:** Your puppy is the 9-to-5er, the hardworking dog who lives to work. Give this dog a job, and he's content.

- **3, 11, 19:** Your puppy is the boss, best known as the Don. This type of dog is nothing if she's not alpha, and she must be reminded she's not the boss of everyone, especially you.

- **4, 12, 20:** Your puppy is the Lone Ranger, the aloof, independent type of dog who looks beautiful and knows it.

- **5, 13, 21:** Your puppy is the Wallflower. This shy pup needs time to warm up to new people and situations, but just because he's a bit introverted doesn't mean he's not rich with personality.

- **6, 14, 22:** Your puppy is the Couch Potato. Lazy days and soft couches make this slow-moving dog feel like he's in heaven.

- **7, 15, 23:** Your puppy is the Jock, the ever-moving, always jumping athlete. Agility, fly ball, jogging, and just about any sport you can think of make Jocks joyful.

- **8, 16, 24:** Your puppy is the Diva or the Pretty Boy, usually smaller-breed dogs that are good-looking, perfectly groomed, and believe their owners are there to do their bidding.

THE

CHEERLEADER

Cheerleaders embody all that is good about dogs: playfulness, loyalty, silliness, and overall joy. Constantly happy, Cheerleaders are the types of dogs everyone wants to have in the family. They greet you enthusiastically when you come in, have goofy "grins" on their faces, wag their tails to excess, and would rather play with you than just about anything else. They're like eternally innocent, sweet,

MOST COMMON breeds

American pit bull terrier, beagle, Boston terrier, boxer,
Cavalier King Charles spaniel, cocker spaniel, Dalmatian, French bulldog,
golden retriever, Jack Russell terrier, Labrador retriever, pug

and curious four-year-olds. Cheerleaders are neither hyper nor dull, aggressive nor shy. They're the even-keeled, happy-go-lucky canine most of us picture when we think of dogs. Coming in a variety of shapes and sizes, Cheerleaders usually sport easy-to-manage coats topping their sturdy, medium- to large-framed bodies. They bark out of sheer joy and often get so excited when you arrive home that they bowl you over and lick you clean. Everything is fun to these Cheerleaders, even going to the mailbox or examining a bug, as long as they're with you. Each day is like Christmas morning to these perky pups, and their joie de vivre is infectious.

 NAMES

Cheerleaders need friendly names that illustrate their zest for life. These monikers are happy, joyful, the epitome of pleasure and fun. Try smiling when you say some of these names—or better yet, try *not* smiling as you say them. Sometimes, the meanings are what make these names Cheerleader-worthy, while others just sound as if they belong to a perky, peppy, pom-pom'ed performer on the football field. Yet all are appropriate for these antidepressant pups that bring light into our lives and joy into our hearts.

Abby—Happy

Allegra—Joy

Allie—Kind, noble

Alyssa—Logical

Amber—Gorgeous and golden

Andi—Casual

Andy—Manly

Angie—Messenger of God

Annie—Gracious, merciful

Archie—Truly bold

Asher—Happy, blessed

Ashley—Woodland sprite

Ashlyn—Natural

Auggie—Determined

Bailey—Attentive

Bart—Hill

Beatrix—Happy

Bonnie—Good

Brandy—Bold

Brittney—From Britain

Buffy—Plains dweller

Calliope—Beautiful voice

Candie—Bright, sweet

Caroline—Beautiful woman

Casey—Attentive

Cassidy—Clever

Cassie—Insightful

Charlie—Free man

Chelsea—Safe harbor

Chloe—Verdant and blooming

Clemmie—Gentle, merciful

Cooper—Handsome

Courtney—Regal

Crosby—Easygoing

Daisy—Daisy flower

Dana—Bright gift of God

Delaney—Bouncy, enthusiastic

Dempsey—Respected

Dixon—Happy

Dorian—Happy

Dosia—Happy

Dotty—Spunky

Dusty—Brave

Dylan—Creative

Eddie—Prosperous

CONTINUES ON PAGE 22

TOP skills FOR PUPPIES

TEACHING basic obedience skills is a great thing to do with your puppy right away. Remember to be patient and proceed slowly with commands. Dogs thrive on routine, so be consistent with your training. Always focus on positive reinforcement, not negative punishment, when teaching these four top skills.

SIT Hold a small, high-value treat (like a piece of cooked liver or cheese) in front of your puppy's nose, then move it up so her focus follows the treat's movement. Eventually, she'll sit down in order to keep her eye on the morsel. As she sits, say "sit," issue praise using her name, and then offer the treat. Do it again and again, and eventually she'll sit when she sees the treat.

LIE DOWN Have your puppy move from a sitting position down to the ground by holding a treat in front of her nose and moving it to the floor. Say "down," then praise her when her belly is on the floor. Reward her with the treat.

STAY Use the leash for this one. Place your puppy in a sitting position, hold your hand in front of her face, and say "stay" while you hold the leash with the other hand and stand in front of her. Take one step back. Wait a second or two, then say "good stay." Praise and treat. With consistent practice, you'll be able to increase the amount of time she'll stay put.

COME Go into another room, then tell your puppy to "come," and use her name. When she reaches you, praise her enthusiastically, treat her, and say "good come!"

Elise—My God is a vow

Eliza—Sworn to God

Ella—Bright light

Ellie—Light

Elvis—All wise

Emily—Poised

Farrell—Courageous

Felice—Happy

Felicia—Happy

Felix—Happy, lucky

Fletch—Arrow maker

Frankie—Free man

Freddie—Peace

Fritz—Peace

Gallagher—Eager helper

Gayleen—Happy

Gemma—Jewel

Gibson—Smiling

Gilligan—Lad

Gilo—Joyful

Goldie—Bright and golden girl

Gracie—Goodwill

Hannah—Merciful

Hayley—Hero

Henry—Ruler of the home

Hobbs—Intelligent

Hopper—Resourceful

Iggy—Spunky

Indigo—Eyes of deep blue

Issac—Laughter

Jack—Personality-plus

Jackie—Personable

Jay—Colorful

Jeffrey—God's peace

Jenny—Beautiful perfection

Jeremy—Talkative

Jessie—Friendly

Jimmy—Dependable

Jody—God adds

Joy—Joy

Justin—Fair

Kadie—Virtuous

Kailah—Virtuous

Kailey—Spunky

Kaitlyn—Pure-hearted

Kallan—Loving

Kara—Friend

Kasem—Joyful

Katie—Pure

Keaton—Nature lover

Kelly—Brave

Kelsey—Opinionated

Kip—Focused

Kitty—Pure

Kory—God's peace

Kylie—Graceful

Lacey—Cheery

Lexie—Sparkling

Libby—God's oath

Lily—Lily

Liza—Smiling

Lizzy—God's oath

Lolly—Sweet

Lucy—Light

Mackenzie—Leader

Maddox—Giving

Maggie—Child of light

Makena—Happy one

Mandy—Worthy of love

Marjie—Pert

Marley—Attractive

May—Great

Maya—Divine creative force in everything

Megan—Precious, joyful

Meggi—Precious, joyful

Melanie—Sweet

Melody—Songlike

Mickey—Enthusiastic

Mikey—Who is like God

Miles—Forgiving

Missy—Honey

Molly—Jovial

Monty—Handsome

Murray—Sailor

Nandi—Happy, joyful

Natalie—Born on Christmas Day

Nellie—Most beautiful woman

Nikki—Winning

Ollie—Loving nature

Owen—Young fighter

CONTINUES ON PAGE 26

GROOMING 101

For people, bathing is an enjoyable daily ritual. But for our favorite four-legged pals, a warm bath does not always equal bliss. Introducing your new puppy to proper grooming techniques early on helps set the stage for a lifetime of pleasant, hassle-free baths.

Begin by gently **WIPING YOUR PUP'S FEET**, ears, face, tail, and nose with a soft, dry towel. Run a brush down his back and play with his feet. Stay positive and keep it short. Do this for a few days until he gets accustomed to the brush and towel.

When he's ready, brush your pup to loosen hair and feel for cuts or lumps requiring veterinary attention. Use age- and breed-appropriate **TOOLS;** when you bathe him, keep in mind that human products are not formulated for dogs, and only dog shampoo and conditioner should be used to lather him up. Place your puppy in a towel-lined sink or tub. Rinse with **WARM WATER,** keeping the nozzle close to his body. Use a damp washcloth on his face and the exterior parts of his ears. Lather front to back, and rinse more than you think you need to. When you feel you're done, rinse again. Apply conditioner, if necessary, and rinse repeatedly. Dry him with a cotton towel, paying close attention to ears and eyes. **TRIM** each nail, holding his paw in one hand and clippers in the other. Place clippers over the nail and clip only the tip. (Ask your vet or a professional groomer to show you how to do this if you're unsure—cutting too much nail can be painful to the dog.) Use a gauze-wrapped finger or special dog toothbrush with canine toothpaste to gently massage your puppy's teeth and gums.

Above all, stay **CALM** and **ASSERTIVE** when grooming your dog. Make it positive, and keep your sense of humor. Both of you will most likely be wet, but happy and clean, at the end of bath time.

Ozzie—Divine power

Penny—Spunky

Perdita—The lost

Phoebe—The shining one

Piper—Musical

Pippa—Ebullient

Polly—Joyous

Poppy—Bouncy girl

Presley—Talented

Quincy—Patient

Reggie—King

Ricky—Powerful, strong ruler

Riley—Courageous, lively

Robbie—Brilliant

Romy—Roaming

Ronni—Energetic

Rori—Spirited

Rosie—Blushing beauty

Roxie—Lovely as the sun

Rusty—Charmer

Sally—Princess

Sam—Good listener

Satchel—Unique

Savannah—Open heart

Seeley—Happy, fortunate

Shay—Bolstering

Shelby—Established

Shelly—Meadow on a hilltop

Shiloh—Gift from God

Sidney—Attractive

Sierra—Outdoorsy

Skippy—Fast

Sophie—Wisdom

Stella—Star

Suki—Beloved

Susie—Pretty flower

Tammi—Sweetheart

Tate—To be cheerful

Tatum—Brings joy

Taylor—Tailor

Terry—Tender, gracious

Tiffany—Lasting love

Tilly—Cute

Timmy—Honoring God

Toby—The Lord is good

Torie—Victory

Tracy—Wild

Trixie—Bringer of joy

Tucker—Stylish

Umi—Life

Vali—Brave man

Vanessa—Flighty

Wally—Charming

Wendy—Fair one

Woody—Jaunty

Wylie—Charmer

Wymer—Rambunctious

Wyton—Crowd-pleaser

Xavier—Shining

Xaxon—Happy

Yue—Happy

Yukio—Happy man

Zack—Spiritual

Zavion—Smiling

Zeke—Friendly, outgoing

Zelig—Happy

Ziggy—Zany

Zoey—Life

Zoltan—Lively

Zorby—Tireless

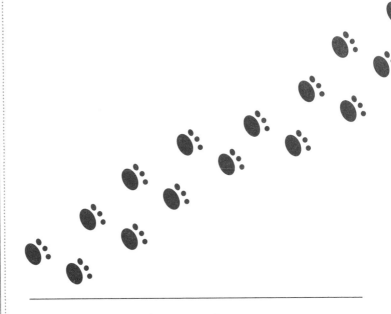

Presidential **NAMES**

These men may each have been commander in chief,
but at some point during their terms as president of the
United States, every one of them answered to a dog—
usually while playing fetch on the White House lawn or
distributing treats in the Oval Office.

George Washington—Drunkard, Mopsey, Taster, Cloe, Tipsy, Tipler, Forester, Captain, Lady Rover, Vulcan, Sweetlips, Searcher

Abraham Lincoln—Fido, Jip

Theodore Roosevelt—Pete, Skip, Blackjack, Manchu, Rollo, Sailor Boy

Warren Harding—Laddie Boy, Old Boy

Calvin Coolidge—Rob Roy, Peter Pan, Paul Pry, Prudence Prim, Calamity Jane, Blackberry, Tiny Tim, Ruby Rough, Boston Beans, King Kole, Bessie, Palo Alto

Herbert Hoover—Big Ben, Eaglehurst Gillette, Glen, King Tut, Patrick, Yukon, Sonnie, Weejie, Pat

Franklin D. Roosevelt—Fala, Major, Meggie, President, Blaze, Tiny, Wink

Harry S. Truman—Feller, Mike

Dwight D. Eisenhower—Heidi

John F. Kennedy—Charlie, Pushinka, Butterfly, White Tips, Blackie, Streaker, Shannon, Wolf, Clipper

Lyndon B. Johnson—Blanco, Her, Him, Yuki

Richard Nixon—Checkers, King Timahoe, Pasha, Vicky

Gerald Ford—Liberty

Ronald Reagan—Lucky, Rex

George H. W. Bush—Millie, Ranger

Bill Clinton—Buddy

George W. Bush—Barney, Spot, Miss Beazley

9-TO-5ER

All work and no play makes Jack a dull boy, huh?
Not for these working dogs, best known as 9-to-5ers. These pups thrive for jobs; nothing pleases them more in this world than having a task. The 9-to-5ers are a very intelligent bunch, almost incredibly so, and they promise to challenge most any owner with their mental acuity. They can learn to do amazing things, like herd a flock of sheep, sniff out

MOST COMMON breeds

Australian cattle dog, Australian shepherd, border collie, Australian kelpie, collie, Anatolian shepherd, German shepherd, rottweiler, Belgian Malinois, Shetland sheepdog, Old English sheepdog, English springer spaniel, Siberian husky, Alaskan malamute, Bouvier des Flandres, Queensland heeler, komondor bombs, and rescue people. Working dogs can put in a full day at the "office," come home, grab a few minutes of shut-eye, and awake refreshed to work once more. Their stamina and dogged determination make 9-to-5ers true assets. Most dogs falling under this personality type are sturdily built, medium to large in stature with dense, all-weather, double-layered coats. Big ears are also seen on many 9-to-5ers, as are lean body frames and thick tails. Clear, almost humanlike eyes study every movement, every detail of their surrounding world. Of course, there are exceptions to the physical description, like the rottweiler, with his small ears and short coat. But all possess the most important characteristic of the 9-to-5er—the ability to focus completely on the job at hand. Working dogs require daily activity, or else hyperactivity, naughty behaviors, and neurotic tics like incessant chewing and pacing may result. A busy 9-to-5er is one happy worker bee.

NAMES

Working dogs don't have time for flowery, multisyllabic names. They don't want to waste a moment of productive daylight waiting for you to finish pronouncing their names. These 9-to-5ers need no-nonsense, meaty, salt-of-the-earth names that get the job done. Just like these dogs do.

Abner—Cheerful leader

Aengus—Exceptionally strong

Akika—Works with determination

Akila—Intelligent

Alice—Noble

Amalea—Hardworking

Amalie—Industrious, striving

Amelita—Hardworking

Amerigo—Hardworking

Amery—Divine, work rule

Asiel—The work of God

Ayita—Worker

Ayman—Lucky

Baird—Creative

Baldric—Leader

Barb—Stranger

Beau—Handsome

Beauvis—Handsome face

Beowulf—Intelligent wolf

Berto—Intelligent

Betty—God's oath

Beverly—Friendly

Brantley—Proud

Brawley—Meadow man

Brenda—Sword

Brian—Strong man of honor

Buck—Cowboy

Calvin—Bold

Carol—Champion

Clara—Bright, clear

Clifton—Risk taker

Clint—Bright

Clyde—Warm

Conan—Intelligent

Dallas—Wise

Dalton—Farmer

Dan—God is my judge

Darren—Great

Darryl—Beloved

Dean—Calming

Dell—Noble

Dennis—Reveler

Dex—Hearty

Dextra—Skilled

Dinah—Vindicated

YOUR first DAY HOME

There are few things in life more exciting than bringing home a new puppy. It's bound to be a bit chaotic at times, but by following a few guidelines, establishing consistently enforced rules, and remaining calm, you are setting the stage for a happy life together.

First, create **HOUSE RULES** before even visiting the breeder. Do you want the dog to sleep on your bed? Potty in only one area of the yard? Never beg for food at the dinner table? Figure out your rules and stick to them. This ensures fewer problems later on because your pup will learn the right behavior from the start.

Bring your puppy home during a **CALM TIME** in your life, not on Christmas Eve or the night before your son's graduation party. Do it on a Friday so you have the weekend to settle in. If you have dogs already, introduce them on neutral territory, and ask your breeder for advice. When you get home, take your puppy outside on a leash and let him explore. Encourage and wait for him to potty, then go inside. Keep him on a leash or follow him very closely while he investigates the house and crate. Show him his water and food bowls.

Make sure the pup is always **IN SIGHT** and out of harm's way. You wouldn't let a two-year-old have free run throughout your house, would you? Same rules apply with a puppy. When you can't watch him, put him in his crate or in a safely fenced-off area, like a bathroom or kitchen. Make sure to remove any chewing temptations first, though.

Above all, **PRAISE** your new puppy often, stay calm, and give lots and lots of **LOVE**.

Dixie—From the south

Donna—Lady

Doreen—Golden

Dorothy—Gift of God

Duane—Little dark one

Dustin—Valiant fighter

Earl—Nobleman

Elaine—Light

Elpaal—God's work

Emelin—Hardworking

Emeric—Leader

Emery—Ruler of work

Emmeline—Industrious

Emmett—Hard worker

Emmy—Hard worker

Ena—Intense

Ethel—Noble

Fabrice—Works with his hands

Ferron—Ironworker

Garrison—Sturdy

Garth—Garden keeper

Georgia—Farmer

Gilson—Devoted son

Gloria—Glory

Griffin—Unconventional

Harsha—Workmanship

Hayne—Working outdoors

Helen—Light

Ida—Hardworking

Idania—Hardworking

Idetta—Hard worker

Idette—Hard worker

Idone—Hard worker

Janet—Forgiving

Janice—God is gracious

Jed—Friend of God

Jedi—Beloved of God

Jedrick—A strong man

Jedrus—Strong

Jim—One who supplants

Joe—God adds

John—God is gracious

Judd—Praised

Kalei—One who works for the king

Kay—Pure

Kazi—Work

Kellagh—Hardworking

Kincade—Vigorous

Kynan—Leads

Laura—Laurel

Laverne—Springlike

Lee—Field

Leona—Lion

Loretta—Large-eyed beauty

Lynn—From the lake

Macon—Creative

Maxima—Miracle worker

Mel—Mill worker

Melia—Work

Melva—Mill worker

Melvin—Friendly

Milia—Hard worker

Milica—Work

Miller—Mill worker

Millicent—Strong work

Milman—Mill worker

Myra—Admirable

Nancy—Grace

Nate—Magnanimous

Necie—Intense

Niles—Smooth

Norma—Rule

Obed—A workman

Orino—Workman's meadow

Ovid—Worker

Paul—Small

Paula—Little

Prue—Intelligent, cautious

Queta—Head of the house

Radilu—Works for the people

Rambert—Mighty, intelligent

Rona—Powerful

Roscoe—Nature-loving

Ruff—Red-haired

Sage—Prophet

Sawyer—Woodworker

Sharon—Princess

Shirley—Country meadow

Spicer—One who works with spices

Tanner—Leather worker

CONTINUES ON PAGE 41

Cosmopolitan **NAMES**

Dogs today have ancestry that hails from countries all over the world, such as the French bulldog, Irish wolfhound, Black Russian terrier, Chinese shar-Pei, Italian greyhound, German shepherd, Greek harehound, and Spanish water dog. Why not pick a cultural name to enhance the heritage of your pup?

AFRICAN

Halla—Unexpected gift

Kia—Season's beginning

Paki—Witness

Pita—Fourth daughter

Moswen—Light in color

Zareb—Protector

CHINESE

Cheung—Good luck

Ciana—God is gracious

Jing-Quo—Ruler of the country

Keung—Universe

Ling—Dainty

Manchu—Pure

Mei—Great

Yin—Silver

FRENCH

Alaire—Joyful

Antoinette—Praiseworthy

Babette—Stranger

Chevalier—Knight

Gerard—Brave

Mardi—Born on a Tuesday

Montague—Pointed mountain

Pierre—Small rock

GERMAN

Alphonese—Noble and eager

Eginhard—Power of the sword

Etta—Little

Grisel—Gray woman warrior

Hilda—Armored warrior

Ludwig—Famous warrior

Meinhard—Strong

Otto—Rich

GREEK

Adonis—Highly attractive

Agamemnon—Resolute

Anastacia—Resurrection

Christos—Christ bearer

Demetria—Cover of the earth

Demos—Of the people

Kyros—Master

Odysseus—Wrathful

Persephone—Springtime

Philomena—Love song

Zorba—Live each day

IRISH

Catelyn—Pure

Cormac—Raven's son

Keera—Dark

Liam—Determined guardian

Lochlain—Land of lakes

Maloney—Church-going

Moira—Great

Roarke—Famous ruler

Tierney—Lordly

ITALIAN

Angelo—Angel

Bianca—White

Chiara—Bright

Dominico—Belonging to the Lord

Gianna—God is gracious

Gino—Born to nobility

Paolo—Small

Pia—Devout

Vincenzo—Conqueror

RUSSIAN

Alek—Brilliant

Aloysha—Defends mankind

Anya—Gracious

Bogdan—Gift from God

Dema—Calm

Igor—Warrior of peace

Katerina—Pure

Michail—Who is like God

Oleg—Holy

Svetlana—Star

SPANISH

Alejandra—Defender of mankind

Bernardo—Brave as a bear

Carlos—Farmer

Conseuelo—Consolation

Corazón—Heart

Lorenzo—Crowned with laurel

Paquita—Free

Paz—Peaceful

Pedro—Small rock

Telfer—Works in iron

Tess—To reap

Tom—A twin

Trudy—Hopeful

Turner—Woodworker

Tyron—Self-reliant

Usher—Decisive

Uso—Intelligent

Veto—Intelligent

Vine—Vineyard worker

Wanda—Kindred

Wayne—Wagon driver

Wilfred—Peaceful

Wilmot—Touch-minded

Wright—Clear-minded

Xandra—Protective

Yenge—Work

Zeb—Gift from God

GET YOUR PUP
TO LEARN HIS name

After much soul searching and research, you've done it—found the perfect name for your new puppy. Now how can you get him to recognize it? It's vital that your new pup learn his name quickly. Start by using it as often as possible. Say, "Here's your toy, Jack," "Time to eat, Jack," "Let's go outside, Jack," and "Come here, Jack." Use his name every time you praise him, pet him, and feed him—and say it with a happy tone in your voice. Repetition is clearly the key. Then, reward him with praise for responding to his name.

TRY THIS: When your pup is engaged in something else and not looking at you, say his name in a normal voice. As soon as he looks up to determine the source of the noise, say, "Good boy, Jack," and offer him a yummy treat. Repeat often until he consistently looks at you when he hears his name. As he gets better, try this exercise in the distraction-filled backyard. Never use your puppy's name when you scold him, and don't ever yell his name in anger, either. You want your pup to associate his moniker with good things, not fear or punishment.

DON

Many of us survived our schoolyard bullies and became accomplished, self-confident adults only to answer to . . . our dogs? Yes, bossy dogs. The Don. First rule of Club Don: There is only one boss, and you're looking at her. Second rule of Club Don: Refer to the first rule.

These dogs call the shots. They come in all shapes and sizes, male and female, little and big. Dons bark. A lot. They

MOST COMMON breeds

Irish terrier, schipperke, German shepherd, Scottish terrier, miniature pinscher, Siberian husky, Pembroke Welsh corgi, rat terrier, Akita, cane corso, rottweiler, Doberman

paw to get your attention, charge out the front door, order you around, and basically scream, "I am alpha!" every chance they get. This is not to say Dons are aggressive. No, they're just right about everything, all the time. And they love letting you know it. They are sweet and kind—until someone questions their authority. Then they, in no uncertain terms, explain the rules. Dons are also smart dogs, almost frighteningly so. They enjoy mentally challenging their owners, and for this reason might be tough to train. But once they catch on, there's no stopping them. Many Dons are extremely obedient, so long as they are reminded that the owners are the boss of them, and not vice versa. It takes an experienced, or at least strong-minded, owner to successfully manage a Don, but it's not to say these skills cannot be learned. After all, what great relationship didn't take a bit of work to become truly rewarding? Just make sure to show up daily, on time, and don't forget to clock in. After all, the boss is watching.

As with any boss, Dons require powerful names, ones that resonate respect and command attention, illustrate their brains and accomplishments. Think of what you'd name a child if you wanted him or her to grow up and run a Fortune 500 company. That's the kind of name Dons desire. You'll find no Blossoms or Baileys here. It's doubtful Dons would even answer to anything less than steely, strong, and formidable. Heck, they might even fire you.

BOSS

Adlai—Refuge of God

Alan—Handsome boy

Alasdai—Defender of man

Alexander—Great leader

Andreas—Brave

Andrew—Manly and brave

Angelo—Messenger

Anne—Full of grace, loving

Archard—Bold

Arnulfo—Strong

Augustin—Magestic

Aza—Powerful

Balthasar—God save the king

Barak—Success

Barton—Persistant man

Baudoin—Winning

Bernard—Bold as a bear

Brad—Expansive

Bradford—Mediator

Braxton—Worldly

Bruce—Complicated

Cameron—Mischievous

Candace—Glowing

Cannon—Courageous

Carl—Kingly

Carson—Confident

Carvell—Innovative

Cesar—Leader

Charles—Strong

Chava—Life

Chynna—Wise

Colin—Victor

Condoleeza—Smart

Constance—To be knowledgeable

Cordelia—Heart

Corin—Combative

Cowell—Brash

Cyril—Regal

Dalt—Abundant

Damian—To tame

Darold—Clever

Davida—Beloved

Diane—Divine

Dirk—Leader

Donald—World leader

CONTINUES ON PAGE 52

Famous **PEOPLE'S DOGS**

The rich and famous may live lives quite different from the average person's, but when it comes to loving dogs, everyone is on the same page. From unusual to silly, average to over-the-top, the names these celebrities have chosen for their beloved pups span the spectrum.

Arthur—ELTON JOHN

Atticus Finch and **Boo Radley**—JAKE GYLLENHAAL

Baci and **Petals**—SIGOURNEY WEAVER

Bella and **Bearlie**—JUSTIN TIMBERLAKE

Bianca Romijn-Stamos-O'Connell—HOWARD STERN

Bing, Bong, and **Jack**—MARIAH CAREY

Blue and **George**—DAVID DUCHOVNY

Blue Maximillian Chow Chow Chow, Genghis Khan Chin-Chin, Kublai Khan Paw Paw Chow Chow Chow, Sharkey, Francesca, Empress Wu, and **Zu-Zu**—MARTHA STEWART

Bob, Kernie, April, Poppy, and **Ruby** —SANDRA BULLOCK

Bubba—MINNIE DRIVER

Buttermilk and **Shug** —ASHLEY JUDD

Centaur Pendragon, Prince, and **Kabar** —RUDOLPH VALENTINO

Chiquita—MADONNA

Clancy—DENIS LEARY

Clara Bo—KATE HUDSON

Commissioner—CLARK GABLE AND CAROL LOMBARD

Daisy—JESSICA SIMPSON

Delilah, Denver, and **Tucker**—CHARLIZE THERON

Duke—JOHN WAYNE

Dylan and **Woof** —RENÉE ZELLWEGER

Esther—FRAN DRESCHER

Fionula and **Whitey** —BILLY JOEL

Frank Sinatra, Coco Chanel, and **Chi Chi Rodriguez**—REESE WITHERSPOON

George—JIM CARREY

Henry—ISAAC MIZRAHI

Holden—GWYNETH PALTROW

Hopper—COURTENEY COX

Hugo, Tippy, and **Muggsie**—MARILYN MONROE

Indo and **Zhaki**—WILL SMITH

Joey and **Raven**—LEANN RIMES

Judas—JARED LETO

Junior—LUCILLE BALL

Karu—HILARY SWANK

Lola—HILARY DUFF

Loretta Lynn—WYNONNA JUDD

Lucy—JODIE FOSTER

Marley—JOHN GROGAN

Martha—PAUL MCCARTNEY

Matzoball—ADAM SANDLER

Mimi La Rue—TORI SPELLING

Miss Hud
—MATTHEW MCCONAUGHEY

Mr. Famous—AUDREY HEPBURN

Norman—JENNIFER ANISTON

Orson—JON KATZ

Poppy—TIM BURTON

Porgy and **Bess**—JUDE LAW

Puggy Sue—PAULA ABDUL

Raleigh—CLAY AIKEN

Rufus—WINSTON CHURCHILL

Sally—MATTHEW BRODERICK
AND SARAH JESSICA PARKER

Sammy—BARBRA STREISAND

Samson—ALICIA SILVERSTONE

Scout—SHERYL CROW

Sid and **Nancy**—JESSICA ALBA

Sluggo—COMEDIAN RON WHITE

Sophie and **Solomon**
—OPRAH WINFREY

Sui—STEVE IRWIN

Talullah Bighead
—JUDD NELSON

Templeton, Flossie, and
Vivian—DREW BARRYMORE

Tinkerbell—PARIS HILTON

Trixie—DEAN KOONTZ

Winston—GWEN STEFANI AND
GAVIN ROSSDALE

Wolf Fishbein—BRUCE WILLIS

Zero—HUMPHREY BOGART

Duke—Leader

Dyna—Powerful

Edgar—Success

Eleanor—Light

Eliseo—Daring

Ellery—Dominant

Emerson—Able

Evan—Warrior

Eve—Life

Fallon—In charge

Favianna—Confident

Ford—Strong

Franklin—Outspoken

Gavin—Alert

Gellert—Powerful soldier

Geneva—Flourishing like juniper

Giann—Believer in a gracious God

Grant—Expansive

Grayson—Son of the gray-haired one

Guido—Guiding

Gunnar—Bold

Gwen—Bright

Harrison—Adventurer

Hillary—Outgoing

Hudd—Powerful

Hudson—Charismatic adventurer

Ignatius—Firebrand

Imelda—Warrior

Indira—Bestower of wealth

Indra—God of power

Jada—Personable

James—Steadfast

Jefferson—Dignified

Jerard—Confident

Jerome—Blessed

Joachim—Powerful

Joan—God's gracious gift

Jordan—Descending

Jovan—Gifted

Judith—Woman worthy of praise

Kacondra—Bold

Kana—Powerful, strength of character

Kane—Warrior

Karian—Daring

Karsten—Chosen one

Kat—Outrageous

Kellan—Powerful

Kennedy—Leader

Kenward—Bold

Kenyon—Blond-haired

Kingston—Gracious

Kirk—Believer

Leander—Brave man

Lincoln—Lithe

Lochlain—Assertive

Lorcan—Little fierce one

Luther—Famous warrior

Maldon—Strong and combative

Maria—The perfect one

Marian—Bitter

Mariel—The perfect one

Marlaina—Dramatic

Marsha—Combative

Marshall—Giving care

Marston—Personable

Martha—Lady

Mather—Powerful army

Matilda—Power

Meg—Strong, able

Meredith—Protector

Meryl—Well known

Milton—Innovative

Mina—Willful

Mitch—Optimist

Mordecai—Combative

Nico—Victor

Nina—Bold girl

Omar—Spiritual

Oprah—Gold

Orlando—Renowned in the land

Othello—Bold

Otto—Wealthy

Pablo—Strong

Patton—Brash warrior

CONTINUES ON PAGE 56

HOW to take **GREAT PUPPY PICTURES**

Like a new baby, puppies are just too cute not to document with hundreds of photographs. Puppies grow remarkably fast, so you'll want to capture these moments before they pass. Yet unlike newborn babies, puppies do not often stay still long enough to snap a perfect photo. Don't despair— with a little bit of know-how, you can have enough photos of your canine companion to fill many scrapbooks.

- Photograph your puppy while he's **NAPPING**. Zoom in on his features, like his nose and paws.

- Use an **ASSISTANT** to hold the puppy.

- Utilize **TREATS** or call your pup's name to capture his attention as you press the shutter.

- Take photos **OUTSIDE** to avoid that "glowing eye" quality created by the flash.

- Try photographing your pup just before his dinner, so you have his attention with treats. Or do it when he's **SLEEPY** and less energetic.

- Always carry a camera with you so you can take those classic **CANDID** shots. Don't worry about being professional. Just have fun.

- Capture your pup's personality by **OBSERVING** and photographing, not involving yourself in the shot or trying to dictate your pup's actions.

- Get down on your **KNEES** or belly when shooting photos.

- Avoid **DISTRACTING** backgrounds.

- Get **CLOSE** up.

- And don't forget to place photos on a picture-sharing website, or make your own website for your pampered prince or princess.

Prescott—Sophisticated

Preston—Spiritual

Quinn—Wise

Randolf—Wise power

Raymond—Strong

Raynard—Sly

Raynor—Strong counselor

Reese—Ardent, fiery

Regan—Nobility

Reinhart—Brave-hearted

Reinhold—A wise and powerful ruler

Remington—Intellectual

Renee—Reborn

Rex—Kingly

Rhona—Powerful, mighty

Richman—Has power

Richmond—Strong protector

Rick—Powerful; strong ruler

Roark—Ruler

Roberta—Bright fame

Rodina—Famous, powerful ruler

Roger—Famed warrior

Roldan—Powerful, mighty

Roy—King

Rush—Loquacious

Ryker—Powerful ruler

Sabin—Daring

Samara—Watchful

Sanford—Negotiator

Sarita—Regal

Sigourney—Leader who conquers

Sinbad—Daring

Slade—Child of the valley

Stephen—Crown

Strider—Great warrior

Stuart—Watchful

Synpha—Capable

Talia—Golden

Thaddeus—Courageous

Thor—Protective

Thorne—Complex

Tien—First and foremost

Tillman—Leader

Tova—Good

Truman—Faithful man

Ulrich—Ruling, powerful

Vala—Powerful

Valdemar—Famous ruler

Vanya—Self-assured

Varlan—Tough

Victor—Conqueror

Viggo—Exuberant

Vincent—Victor

Walker—Distinctive

Walter—Powerful warrior

Walther—Powerful ruler

Willem—Resolute guardian

Wistar—Respected

Wolfgang—Talented

Xerxes—Leader

Yianni—Creative

York—Affluent

Zane—God's gracious gift

Safety **PRECAUTIONS**

Getting a new puppy means it's time to puppy-proof your home. Taking safety precautions around the house is time well spent. Crawl on the floor and see what tantalizing goodies lurk—exposed electrical cords, wooden knickknacks, toys, coins. Remember, everything tempts these curious canines. Move breakable objects from coffee tables, put away shoes in closed closets, stash chewable items out of reach, and tuck electrical wires behind furniture. In the kitchen, install a childproof lock on cabinets housing cleaning products, and make sure your puppy can't get at any chocolate, raisins, grapes, coffee, alcohol, onions, yeast dough, or anything moldy or spoiled. Exercise extreme caution when using outdoor items like fertilizer, citronella candles, and snail bait, as all of these can make your puppy very sick.

Keep your puppy **WITHIN SIGHT** and reach at all times. Just as children can get into mischief in two seconds flat, so can a puppy. Erect baby gates and barriers to keep your pup out of certain rooms. Use a **DOG CRATE**—a wire mesh or plastic container with enough room to stand and curl up. It's great for minimizing mischief and encouraging housetraining. Buy a good book on crate training and ask your breeder for how-to instructions. Never use the crate for punishment, and make sure it's associated with **POSITIVE EVENTS** (like high-value treats or dinner). A hard plastic crate is also an excellent safety measure when traveling with your puppy, even to the veterinarian's office. Look into **EXERCISE PENS**, which are fencelike enclosures allowing for more, yet still safe, movement and play.

THE
LONE RANGER

Some folks work best on their own and look good doing it. These Lone Rangers are no exception. Appearing aloof, independent, and a bit standoffish without being totally snobby, Lone Rangers are also dignified, graceful, sophisticated, cautious, and sensitive. Companionship is nice but not required for these aristocratic dogs. Lone Rangers are loyal to their owners, but "Velcro dogs" (who stick to

MOST COMMON breeds

Saluki, Afghan hound, pharaoh hound, Sealyham terrier,
Shiba Inu, Irish wolfhound, borzoi, greyhound,
Chow Chow, basenji

your side 24-7) they are not. They don't live to please their owners, but are attuned to human emotions and the tensions within their households.

Ball-chasing and pool-jumping aren't high priorities for these dogs, who look at the world like movie stars, with shiny coats, graceful faces, and elegant gaits. They're more like fashion models than Frisbee chasers. In fact, Lone Rangers, with their aloof personalities and beauty, are like the canine equivalent of cats. Grooming requirements for some Lone Rangers are not for the weak of heart, while others without the longer hair are more easily washed and brushed. Daily exercise is important to maintain their lanky figure, but so is constant obedience training using positive, intelligent methods. This isn't to say Lone Rangers are unloving. Just as cats will purr and rub against your legs, Lone Rangers, too, need love and affection. Just on their own terms.

NAMES

Lone Rangers need dignified, elegant, respectable names to go along with their independent and reserved personalities. It would be almost insulting to these dogs to saddle them with sugary-sweet or cutesy names. The way these names resonate or the meanings they have give these titles power, class, and elegance. It's a perfect combination for the oh-so-polished Lone Ranger.

Adelaide—Of a noble kin

Adrianna—Rich, exotic

Alala—Protected

Amalia—Industrious

Amandine—Beloved

Anastasia—Royal

Anneliese—Gracious

Ansley—Loner

Antonio—Highly praiseworthy

Anwen—Very beautiful

Aphrodite—Goddess of love and beauty

Aquinnah—High land

Artemis—Goddess of the moon

Audon—Alone

Barlow—Hardy

Baron—Noble leader

Bartholomew—Earthy

Bastian—Respected

Benedict—Blessed

Benson—Brave heart

Benvolio—Goodwill

Blanche—White

Blythe—Carefree

Brenton—Forward-thinking

Brynn—Hill

Cabot—Loves the water

Caledonia—Worthy

Calista—Most beautiful

Carmela—Fruitful

Catalina—Pure

Cavender—Emotional

Chantal—A song

Chaucer—Chancellor

Chiara—Famous

Clarissa—Shining and gentle

Cleopatra—Glory of the father

Colette—Victory of the people

Cosette—Victorious

Crystal—A clear, brilliant glass

Daphne—Pretty nymph

Deirdre—Sparkling

Delyth—Neat and pretty

Demario—Bold

Destiny—Fate

CONTINUES ON PAGE 66

Shopping list
FOR NEW OWNERS

Part of the fun of owning a new puppy is shopping for all of the nifty little goodies available for the canine lover. Some are practical, others frivolous, but all add to the joy of being a puppy parent. It's about this time you realize how much a puppy shower, just like a traditional baby shower, would be appreciated!

- **ID TAG** (printed with your phone number and contact information for a nearby friend or family member)

- Flat, adjustable **COLLAR** and six-foot **LEASH** (either nylon or leather)

- **CRATE,** usually wire with removable dividers

- **PLASTIC TRAVEL CRATE**

- **DOG BED** or **PILLOW** (be careful not to place this in the crate until the chewing stage is over; until then, use old towels or sheets)

- **STAIN/ODOR NEUTRALIZER**

- Stainless steel food and water **BOWLS**

- **STORAGE BIN** for food

- **FOOD** (start with food the breeder or rescue group used, then talk to your vet about how to switch brands if you wish)

- **BRUSH, FLEA COMB,** and **SHAMPOO AND CONDITIONING SPRAY** suitable for your puppy's breed

- **NAIL CLIPPERS**

- **BABY GATES**

- **EXERCISE PEN** (used as a large playpen outside or indoors to further confine the puppy while allowing plenty of room for play)

- **DOG LICENSE** (contact animal control in your area)

- **TREATS**

- **TOYS** (hard rubber toys, balls, squeaky stuffed toys, ropes, rubber bones)

- **SCRAPBOOK** for all the photos you'll take

Devin—Poetic

Diantha—Flower, heavenly

Dieter—Army of the people

Dinos—Proud

Dominique—Of God

Dorothea—Gift of God

Elan—Finesse

Elijah—Jehovah is God

Enzo—Winner

Eponine—French horse goddess

Etienne—Crown

Euphemia—Respected

Evadne—Pleasing

Evelina—Lively

Ewan—Young

Fanteen—Clever

Farrah—Beautiful

Felicity—Happy

Fernando—Brave traveler

Ferris—Rock

Flavio—Shining

Flora—Flowering

Fyodor—Divine

Gaston—Stranger

Gatsby—Ambitious

Gawain—Archangel

Gayton—Fair

Gisella—Pledged for service

Givonnah—Loyal, believer

Godfried—God's grace

Grace—Grace

Gretel—Fanciful

Guinevere—Fair one

Gyan—Knowledgeable

Harmon—Dependable

Hayden—Respectful

Hazel—Commander

Heathcliff—Mysterious

Helena—Beautiful

Inez—Lovely

Isabel—Consecrated to God

Isai—Believer

Isis—Supreme goddess

Jacinda—Attractive girl

Jago—Self-assured

Jucinda—Relishing life

Juliet—Loving

Katya—Pure

Kavan—Good-looking

Kavita—Poem

Keera—Dark-skinned

Kellyn—Brave heart

Kesia—Favorite

Killian—Effervescent

Kristof—Christ bearer

Kyla—Lovely

Lachlan—Feisty

Laird—Wealthy landowner

Lane—Secure

Lauren—Laurel

Leila—Born at night

Liv—Life

Lorenzo—Bold and spirited

Madelyn—Strong woman

Madison—Good-hearted

Maeve—Queen

Mallory—Tough-minded, spunky

Manon—Exciting

Margot—Lively

Matin—Gift

Mavis—Singing bird

Miles—Soldier

Moriah—Great one

Narcissus—Vain

Natasia—Gorgeous girl

Neve—Promising princess

Neviah—Worshipful

Olivia—Olive tree

Ophelia—Helper

Paz—Peaceful

Persephone—Breath of spring

Petra—Glamorous

Pia—Devout

Pilar—Worthwhile, pillar of strength

Quisha—Beautiful mind

Rafferty—Abundance

Raquel—Sensual

Remington—Intellectual

Rhiannon—Goddess, intuitive

CONTINUES ON PAGE 70

Biblical **NAMES**

The Bible has long been a source of names rich with meaning. Many people research this text to find strong, historical names for their children. Why not do the same thing for your dog? Scores of these biblical names are quite familiar and common, while others are more unique. Yet all still have their roots deeply planted in the pages of the Bible.

Aaron—Strong

Abel—A breath

Abraham—Father of a multitude

Adam—Of the earth

Bathsheba—Daughter of an oath

Cain—Craftsman

Delilah—Delicate

Dinah—Vindicated

Eden—Delightful

Elijah—The Lord is my God

Elizabeth—God's oath

Emmanuel—God is with us

Esther—Star

Eve—Life

Ezekiel—God will strengthen

Ezra—Help

Gabriel—God is my strength

Gideon—Great warrior

Hannah—Grace

Jericho—Moon city

Jezebel—Follower of idols

Jonah—A dove

Joseph—God will increase

Judah—Praised

Lazarus—God has helped

Levi—Joined

Luke—Light

Malachi—My messenger

Mary—The perfect one

Micah—Humble

Moses—Born of a God

Naomi—Beautiful

Nicodemus—Victory of the people

Noah—Peace

Obadiah—Servant of the Lord

Omar—Long-lived

Rebekah—To tie

Ruth—Friendship

Salome—Peace

Sarah—Princess

Sheba—Seventh daughter

Simon—To be heard

Solomon—Peace

Titus—Giant

Zacharias—The Lord has remembered

Zebediah—Gift from God

Zechariah—Memory of the Lord

Sarafina—Angelic

Schuyler—Shelter, scholar

Shantie—Peace

Shiva—Life and death

Simone—Wise and thoughtful

Sinclair—Admired

Skye—High-minded

Sloane—Strong

Spencer—Keeper

Sutton—Sunny

Syon—Lucky boy

Tamsin—Benevolent

Trenton—Fast-moving

Trinity—Triad

Tyne—Dramatic

Uma—Nation

Uriah—Bright

Uriel—Light, God-inspired

Vania—Gifted

Vartan—Giver of roses

Venezio—Glorious

Whitmore—White

Whittaker—Outdoorsy

Willoughby—Lives with grace

Willow—Free spirit

Winthrop—Winning, stuffy

Wren—Songbird

Wymann—Contentious

Xanthos—Attractive

Xenos—With grace

Ysanne—Graceful

Yseult—Prettiness

Zaire—Brash

Zeno—Stoic

Zephyr—Breezy

Zion—Excellent

FAMOUS cartoon **CANINES**

Some of our most memorable dogs from childhood might not have been real live dogs at all. But to fans everywhere, these dogs are as real as anything.

Astro (*The Jetsons*)

Barfy (*Family Circus* comic strip)

Blue (*Blue's Clues*)

Bruno (*Cinderella*)

Clifford, the Big Red Dog

Dino (*The Flintstones*)

Dogbert (*Dilbert* comic strip)

Earl (*Mutts* comic strip)

Edgar (*For Better or For Worse* comic strip)

Electra (*Cathy* comic strip)

Farley (*For Better or For Worse* comic strip)

Fuzz (*Ziggy* comic strip)

Goofy

Gromit (*Wallace and Gromit* claymation series)

Hot Dog (*Archie* comic series)

Huckleberry Hound

Ladybird (*King of the Hill*)

Marmaduke

Mr. Peabody (*The Rocky and Bullwinkle Show*)

Odie (*Garfield*)

Perdita (*101 Dalmations*)

Pluto

Pongo (*101 Dalmations*)

Santa's Little Helper (*The Simpsons*)

Satchel (*Get Fuzzy* comic strip)

Scooby-Doo

Slinky (*Toy Story*)

Snoopy

Spike (*Peanuts* comic strip)

Underdog

WALLFLOWER

Hearts go out to the shy dog, also known as the Wallflower. These pups need time to warm up to people and situations, and rarely are they willing to venture out solo and try something new. These dogs are not the first to greet new faces at the dog park, nor are they that eager to join in the fun when games begin. They much prefer the comfort of having their beloved owners doing things with

MOST COMMON breeds

whippet, Italian greyhound, Chinese crested dog, toy poodle, Chihuahua, Yorkshire terrier, Brussels griffon them, protecting them in case things turn sour. Thunderstorms and loud noises may frighten Wallflowers under the bed, where only gentle coaxing can urge them out.

Training must be done gently, and positively reinforced socialization is required to help Wallflowers blossom. But this isn't to say these dogs are fragile and fearful— they're just reserved. They're like shy children, who need some time to get their footing. But once they do, they shine. Introducing your Wallflower to new situations may take some time, but by doing it gently and with plenty of praise, you'll go far. Still waters run deep: Wallflowers may be quiet, but that doesn't mean they're not rich with personality.

Many dogs in this category are often small, a bit timid by breed, and prone to having a quiet, reserved nature. They have thin frames and delicate bone structures. Some emit high-pitched barks, while others whine or make no noise at all. Trembling isn't uncommon, either. But make no mistake: Wallflowers come complete with all the tricks and quirks we have grown to know and love about dogs. While they may seem like that sweet, shy kid in class who was afraid to raise her hand even though she knew the answer, Wallflowers are still playful dogs at heart.

NAMES

Names for these endearing dogs need to be as quiet, sweet, and soft as they are. Nothing too loud, too colorful, or just too much for these Wallflowers. Their names should not sound harsh, nor should they convey images of warriors and superheroes! Wallflowers need timeless names that fit them as comfortably as a pair of broken-in slippers. Mix one part coziness, one part unobtrusive nature and you've got the perfect Wallflower name recipe.

ON THE big screen

There may not be Oscars or Emmy awards for dogs, but that doesn't mean pups on the big screen should not be recognized for their acting chops. Why not name your own companion in honor of a famous canine character?

Bandit (*Little House on the Prairie*)

Baxter (*Anchorman*)

Beethoven (from the *Beethoven* films)

Benji

Blue (*Cool Hand Luke*)

Boomer (*Independence Day*)

Brandon (*Punky Brewster*)

Bruiser (*Legally Blonde*)

Buddy (*Air Bud*)

Buster (*The Bodyguard*)

Chance (*Homeward Bound*)

Cherokee (*Scream 3*)

Chopper (*Stand By Me*)

Churchill (*The Water Horse*)

Diesel (*Snow Dogs*)

Digby (*Pushing Daisies*)

Dreyfus (*Empty Nest*)

Duke (*The Beverly Hillbillies*)

Eddie (*Fraiser*)

Edison (*Chitty Chitty Bang Bang*)

Einstein (*Back to the Future*)

Frank (*Men in Black*)

Freeway (*Hart to Hart*)

Harvey (*E.T.*)

Hercules (*The Sandlot*)

Hooch (*Turner and Hooch*)

Jack (*Little House on the Prairie*)

Jerry Lee (*K-9*)

Kerouac (*Down and Out in Beverly Hills*)

Lassie

Lou (*Cats and Dogs*)

Milo (*The Mask*)

Mr. Beefy (*Little Nicky*)

Murray (*Mad About You*)

Nanook (*The Lost Boys*)

Otis (*The Adventures of Milo and Otis*)

Petey (*The Little Rascals*)

Porthos (*Finding Neverland*)

Precious (*Silence of the Lambs*)

Sandy (*Annie*)

Shiloh (*Saving Shiloh*)

Tiger (*The Brady Bunch*)

Toto (*The Wizard of Oz*)

Tramp (*Lady and the Tramp*)

Verdell (*As Good as It Gets*)

Vincent (*Lost*)

Alfeus—Follower

Anya—Grace

Arden—Sincere

Artie—Wealthy

Arwen—Royal maiden

Asra—Pure

Atzel—Reserved

Ballari—Walking quietly

Barnaby—Son of comfort

Barry—Candid

Benita—Lovely

Bertie—Industrious

Bowen—Shy

Bronwen—Dark and pure

Cailen—Gentle

Carys—Love

Charlotte—Petite and feminine

Cian—Old soul

Cicil—Shy

Claire—Smart

Clarence—Bright, clear

Claudette—Persistent

Cormac—Watchful

Cornelia—Practical

Cornelius—Realistic

Coy—Quiet person

Curtis—Courteous, kindhearted

Dabney—Careful

Darwin—Dearest friend

Delilah—Delicate

Doris—Sea

Dorit—Shy

Dortha—Studious

Dryden—Calm

Dumia—Silent

Dunmore—Guarded

Durwood—Home-loving

Elsworth—Pretentious

Emilia—Soft-spirited

Engelbert—Angel-bright

Estelle—Star

Eudora—Cherished

Eugene—Well born

Eugenia—Regal and polished

Eulala—Spoken sweetly

Eustace—Calming

Eustacio—Calm

Ezikiel—God's strength

Fawn—Gentle

Fawna—Soft-spoken

Faye—Light-spirited

Fern—Fern

Fina—Blessed by God

Florence—Prosperous

Forest—Nature lover

Foster—Worthy

Galbraith—Sensible

Gertrude—Beloved

Gilbert—Intelligent

Gillespie—Humble

Gillian—Devout

Gladys—Flower, princess

Glifford—Generous-hearted

Gomer—To complete

Greer—Aware

Greta—Child of light

Grover—Thriving

Gweneth—Blessed

Harper—Artistic

Harriet—Homebody

Harris—Dignified

Heloise—Hearty

Henrietta—Home ruler

Hernley—Easygoing

Hilda—Practical

Imogen—Innocent

Ingram—Kind

Ingrid—Beautiful

Ira—Cautious

Iris—Bright

Irving—Attractive

Irwin—Practical

Isidro—Gift

Jade—Adoring

Janet—Small, forgiving

Jocasta—Cheerful

Julius—Attractive

June—Born in June

Kavi—Poetic

Kermit—Droll

Kiya—Always returning

Kosta—Steady

CONTINUES ON PAGE 82

SOCIALIZING 101

A well-socialized dog is an asset to your home and
community. Often, breeders will have exposed puppies
to basic household stimuli (cars, radios, phones, children,
televisions) from the start. But that doesn't mean the job
is done. Socialization is a work in progress. It's one of the
most important things you can do with your puppy every
day to ensure you're setting up building blocks for a
well-mannered dog that will live a fearless, fulfilling life.

The most convenient time to socialize a pup to new sights, sounds, and experiences is **BEFORE SIXTEEN WEEKS** of age. First, talk to your vet about proper vaccination schedules before taking your pup in public. When you're sure she's up to date on her vaccinations, expose her to new things in a positive, nonthreatening way. Don't force her into situations, and **GO SLOW.** Take her with you everywhere you can, like in the car or to the mall. Place her in a carrier and don't let her near strange dogs or on the ground where dogs have been (like the park). Other dogs and their excrement can carry infections and diseases your young pup's immune system isn't able to fight yet.

Have everyone you meet—old, young, man, woman—give your pup a treat or **KIND GREETING.** Don't leave children alone with your puppy, though. When you get veterinarian's clearance, enroll in a puppy kindergarten obedience class and schedule playdates with healthy puppies. If your pup goes ballistic over a new sight (like a bus), **DON'T OVERREACT** or coddle her. Gently reassure her and divert her attention. Above all, remain calm. She'll remember that next time.

Lennan—Gentle

Lila—Playful

Lilith—Spirit of the night

Linus—Blond

Liu—Quiet

Lloyd—Spiritual

Lorne—Grounded

Louisa—Patient

Lourdes—Hallowed

Lucian—Soothing

Malachy—Messenger of God

Malu—Peaceful

Margaret—Child of light

Mariana—Quiet girl

Marie—The perfect one

Marion—Delicate spirit

Marvin—Friend of the sea

Mildred—Mild strength

Minerva—Bright

Minnie—Loving memory

Moira—Pure

Mona—Solitary

Morris—Dark-skinned

Morrow—Follower

Moses—Appointed for special things

Neville—Innovator

Newton—Bright, new mind

Noah—Peacemaker

Noriko—Follows tradition

Norris—Serious

Olav—Traditional

Ordella—Prays

Oswald—Divine power

Paige—Assistant

Penelope—Patient

Percy—Mysterious

Petunia—Perky

Photius—Scholarly

Phyllis—Beautiful

Placido—Calm, quiet

Prudence—Cautious

Quinby—Living like royalty

Rachelle—Calm

Ramona—Wise

Rose—Rose

Rowan—Little redhead

Rumer—Gypsy

Seamus—Replacement

Sela—A rock

Seymour—Prayerful

Shalev—Quiet, peaceful

Shep—Watchful

Shizo—Quiet

Simeon—Listener

Stanley—Traveler

Stillman—Calm, quiet

Stockley—Rooted in reality

Tace—Silent

Tallulah—Sparkling girl

Tanise—Unique

Thatcher—Practical

Thelma—Giver

Theodora—Sweetheart

Theodore—A blessing

Tiombe—Shy

Tulia—Calm, quiet

Twyla—Creative

Uriela—God's light

Ursa—Star

Ursula—Little female bear

Velma—Hardworking

Veronica—Real

Virginia—Maiden

Vivianna—Inventive

Walton—Shut off, protected

Warren—Safe

Watson—Helpful

Wendell—Wanderer

Wilhelmina—Resolute guardian

Windell—Wanderer

Winifred—Friend of peace

Winston—Winning

Wycliff—Edgy

Xeno—Gracious

Yasuo—Calm

Yemyo—Serene

Yen—Calming

Yianni—Creative

Yoshe—Wise

Zelma—Divine

Blast **FROM THE** past **NAMES**

What's happened to the good, old-fashioned dog names of days gone by? Is it so unusual to have a dog called Spot anymore? If you're a purist and want to take a blast to the past, try one of these classic dog names for your puppy. Who knows? You might set a new trend.

Ace	Bear	Boots	Buster
Bambi	Bebe	Brownie	Champ
Banjo	Bingo	Bubba	Checkers
Barker	Blackie	Bunny	Chief

Chip	Happy	Peanut	Shorty
Coco	Hershey	Pepper	Skipper
Cookie	Huckleberry	Pixie	Smokey
Corky	Ivory	Pluto	Snoopy
Countess	Jaws	Precious	Snowflake
Cupcake	King	Prince	Socks
Daisy	Laddie	Princess	Sounder
Diamond	Lady	Puddles	Spanky
Dolly	Lancelot	Pumpkin	Sparky
Duke	Lassie	Queenie	Spot
Dusty	Licorice	Radar	Squirt
Ebony	Lightning	Ranger	Star
Elmo	Lucky	Red	Sugarpie
Fang	Major	Rocky	Taffy
Fido	Marmaduke	Rover	Tiger
Fluffy	Midnight	Runt	Tinkerbell
Foxy	Muffin	Rusty	Toots
Freckles	Muttley	Sassy	Tootsie
Frenchie	Nugget	Scamp	Tramp
Ginger	Old Yeller	Scooby	Trixie
Goofy	Oreo	Scruffy	Yoda
Gus	Patches	Shadow	
Hairy	Peaches	Shaggy	

6

COUCH POTATO

Ah, the Couch Potato. It's hard not to love these lazy, cuddly, roll-on-their-backs-for-a-belly-rub dogs. Give them a corner of—or the whole—couch, and life is grand. Some believe they're lap dogs despite their size, and all of them love nothing more than a cozy pillow, a gentle pat on the head, and a nearby bowl of food. Calmness reigns, sometimes even during the puppy years, with Couch Potatoes.

 MOST COMMON breeds

basset hound, bloodhound, bull mastiff, Dogue de Bordeaux, Clumber spaniel, English bulldog, Great Pyrenees, greyhound, mastiff, Neapolitan mastiff, Newfoundland, Saint Bernard

These are not the dogs you take running every morning. Sure, Couch Potatoes can and do become excited and animated, but it's usually an isolated event, not an all-day occurrence. They might love to do something strenuous (like cart-pulling Newfoundland-style), but then it's nap time. Sleep is a priority for these pooches, as is a good meal and lots of love. Exercise? Not so much. All a Couch Potato needs is a short walk in the evening, or a game of fetch in the afternoon. When they get older, most of these dogs tire out within minutes, needing a nap to rejuvenate.

Couch Potatoes make great companions for human couch potatoes, too. Think about it: two kindred spirits, sprawled on the sofa, watching sports on a Sunday afternoon, a plate of snacks resting nearby. No drama involved. Couch Potatoes tend to gain weight; they are usually large-boned with thick bodies, big heads, and dense coats. The stubby basset hound and the majestic retired greyhound are common exceptions to this physical description. They might not fit the body type of the Couch Potato, but both embody other character-istics of this personality genre. Couch Potatoes sometimes look intimidating, but they're really pussycats in very large packaging. While they don't bark often, Couch Potatoes command respect when they sound their deep, guttural woof . . . before they roll over and go back to sleep.

Couch Potatoes need easygoing, relaxing, mellow names. While some of the *meanings* may seem to designate a 9-to-5er or Jock, the way they sound is all Couch Potato. When spoken, these names conjure up visions of serenity and lazy days, fleece blankets and fuzzy slippers, hot dogs and rawhide chewies. After all, if it takes too much work to say your Couch Potato's moniker, it's going to be too much work for him to respond to it.

DOG mascots

Sports aficionados are some of the most die-hard
fanatics of the bunch. If you're one of them, choosing
a name that not only suits your puppy but honors your
favorite team might be just the ticket.

Ben—the bulldog mascot of McPherson College

Bully—Mississippi State University's bulldog

Butler Blue II—the bulldog mascot of Butler University

Colonel Rock or Rocky—the bulldog mascot for the Western Illinois University Leathernecks

Duke Dog—the costumed mascot of the James Madison Dukes

George Tirebiter—a stray mutt who became the unofficial mascot of the University of Southern California in the 1940s

Handsome Dan—Yale University's bulldog

Jack the Bulldog—the mascot of Georgetown University's Hoyas

Jonathan—the husky mascot for the University of Connecticut

Q—popular name of Spike Q. Gonzaga, a live bulldog who is one of two official mascots for Gonzaga University

Reveille—the collie mascot for Texas A&M University

Smokey—a bluetick hound that serves as mascot for the University of Tennessee

Spirit—the Alaskan malamute mascot for the University of Washington Huskies

Tech—the bulldog mascot of Louisiana Tech University

Timeout—the costumed bulldog mascot of Fresno State

Uga—the University of Georgia's Bulldog

Zeke the Wonder Dog—the Labrador retriever mascot for Michigan State

Abe—Father of nations

Abel—Vital

Ajax—Of the earth

Aldo—Noble

Algernon—Bearded

Alter—Will live to be old

Alva—Beloved friend

Amos—Strong

Angus—Chosen one

Arlo—Strong

August—Revered, exalted

Barney—Grim bear

Basye—Home-based

Beasley—Nurturing

Beauford—Attractive

Beauregard—A face much admired

Becca—Captivating

Bedrich—Rules peacefully

Ben—Wonderful

Bess—God's oath

Bob—Bright

Bogart—Strong

Boris—One who wins battles

Brennan—Pensive

Bruno—Brown-haired

Brutus—Dull

Chesna—Bringing peace, calm

Chester—Comfy-cozy

Chuck—Strong

Clark—Scholar

Claude—Slow-moving

Clayton—Stodgy

Clem—Casual

Clement—Merciful

Clive—Cliff dweller

Colbert—Cool and calm

Coleman—Peacemaker

Colm—Peaceful

Cora—Filled heart

Corvin—Friend

Costas—Constant

Dantre—Faithful

Dawson—Loved

Della—Kind

Dema—Calm

Dobes—Unassuming

Donahue—Dark warrior

Dora—Gift

Dudley—Stuffy

Dugan—To be worthy

Duncan—Dark-skinned warrior

Dunphy—Serious

Dwight—Intelligent

Ellie—Light

Elliot—The Lord is my God

Elmo—Protector

Erwin—Friendly

Fanny—Free

Fergus—Of manly strength

Finian—Handsome

Finn—Fair

Fitz—Bright young man

Florrie—Blooming

Flossie—Grows beautifully

Flynn—Brash

Frank—A free man

Frannie—Friendly

Fred—Peace

Galen—Calm

Galena—Calm

Garon—Gentle

Garv—Peaceful

Gary—Strong man

Gaylin—Calm

Gentry—Sweet

George—Land-loving

Geraldine—Strong

Gideon—Great warrior

Giffin—Giving

Gifford—Generous-hearted

Glen—Natural wonder

Goliath—Large

Gordon—Triangular-shaped hill

Gulliver—Glutton

Gunter—Battle warrior

Gus—Exceptional

Gustav—Vital

Guthrie—Heroic

CONTINUES ON PAGE 96

TREAT recipes

A home-baked goodie is a real treat, even for our pups. Dog treats are simple and inexpensive to create, and making your own allows you to determine exactly what your dog is eating. Use these recipes, and you'll know she's getting wholesome, nutritious morsels straight from your heart to hers.

FROZEN PEANUT BUTTER YOGURT TREATS

1 cup peanut butter

1 32-ounce container of vanilla yogurt

Place peanut butter in a microwave-safe dish and melt in the microwave on medium heat for 2 minutes. Stir in yogurt. Pour into paper-lined cupcake tins or mini-cupcake containers and freeze. Remove the paper and serve the frozen treats on a hot day.

BAKED BONE TREATS

2 teaspoons dry yeast
2 tablespoons parsley
1 ½ cups chicken broth
3 tablespoons honey

1 egg
5 cups whole-wheat flour
(a bit more if necessary)

Preheat the oven to 350°F. In a large bowl, dissolve yeast in ½ cup of warm water. Stir in the parsley, broth, honey, and egg. Gradually stir in the flour, adding enough to form a stiff dough.

Transfer the dough to a floured surface and knead until smooth, about 3 minutes. Shape the dough into a ball, and roll to ¼-inch thickness. Using small, bone-shaped cookie cutters, or any other cutter shape of your choice, cut out the treats. Gather up the scraps, knead into a ball, roll out the dough, and start the process again until all the dough is used. Transfer the treats to an ungreased baking sheet, spacing them about ¼ inch apart.

Bake for approximately 45 minutes, checking after 20 minutes to make sure the treats are not too brown. After 30 minutes, remove the treats from the oven and turn them over. Bake for an additional 15 minutes or so on the other side, or until lightly browned on both sides. Let the treats cool overnight to get an even crunchier biscuit. These treats freeze well, so make as many as you'd like.

Hank—Ruler of the household

Hardy—Fun-loving

Harry—Home ruler

Hartsey—Lazing on the meadow

Hattie—Home ruler

Homer—Promise

Horace—Poetic

Hubert—Notable person

Hugo—Spirited heart

Humphrey—Peacemaker

Ifan—Believer

Innis—Isolated

Ivan—Reliable one

Jasper—Treasurer

Jeb—Jolly

Jemima—Dove

Jesper—Easygoing

Kasimir—Serene

Keanu—Cool mountain breeze

Kulbert—Calm

Leo—Lion

Liam—Strong-willed warrior

Linfred—Peaceful

Lou—Famed warrior

Louie—Famed in battle

Lucien—Soothing

Luka—Easygoing

Lulu—Soothing, comforting

Lyle—Unique

Mabel—Lovable

Mack—Friendly

Maisie—Treasure

Malana—Relaxing

Malia—Calm and peaceful

Maude—Old-fashioned

Maynard—Reliable

Merle—Shining girl

Milo—Soft-hearted

Moe—Easygoing

Monroe—Delightful

Morgan—Confident

Mungo—Loved

Murphy—Fighter

Nalani—Calmness of the skies

Ned—Prosperous guardian

Nell—Light

Noah—Peace

Nora—Honor

Norm—Sincere

Oded—Supportive

Odin—Soulful

Ogden—From the oak valley

Olive—Olive

Oliver—Eloquent

Orion—Rising in the sky, dawning

Orpheus—Darkness of night

Orson—Bearlike

Oscar—Divine strength

Otis—Intuitive

Pacian—Peaceful

Padraic—Noble

Pasquale—Spiritual

Quita—Peaceful

Radnor—Natural

Ralph—Adviser to all

Redmond—Protective

Reuben—Creative

Rollo—Famed throughout the land

Ross—Wooded meadow

Rowen—Red-haired

Rowena—Famous friend

Rufus—Red

Rumford—Grounded

Rupert—Bright fame

Ruth—Companion, friend

Sadie—Princess

Sakina—Calm, comfort, presence of God

Samson—Strong man

Seaton—Calm

Segenam—Lazy

Seth—Appointed one

Shaw—Safe

Silas—Saver

Siran—Sweet love

Sol—Sun

Solomon—Peace

Stan—Traveler

Thana—Thanksgiving

Theone—Serene

Theophania—God's features

Thora—Like thunder

Ulysses—Wrathful

Violet—Violet flower

Wade—River crossing

Waldo—God's power

Wilber—Willful, bright

Willard—Courageous

Wilson—Extraordinary

Xavion—Home

Yori—Reliable

Zofie—Wise

Funny **NAMES**

Sometimes a "normal" name just won't cut it. Funny names don't have to be cruel (no one really should name their pups Dumb or Stupid), but instead can be clever, original, and always unforgettable.

Beefcake	**Oscar Mayer**
Captain Drool	**Pot Roast**
Deeogee (get it? D-O-G?)	**Rambone**
Diesel	**Salty**
Gidget	**Spuds**
Kemhere (say it fast)	**Tank**
Meatball	**Tater Tot**
Moondoggie	**Twinkie** (for a yellow dog)
Moose	**Zeus** (for a tiny dog)

JOCK

There's something about the Jock that just makes people feel energized. These life-loving, vigor-filled pups are always on the move, eternally looking for the next game of fetch, the next ball to catch, the next hurdle to jump. A quick five-minute nap later, and they're ready to do it all over again. Jocks are like children, full of wonder, energy, and the desire to keep playing long after the sun goes down.

MOST COMMON breeds

American pit bull terrier, Australian shepherd, border collie, Canaan dog, German shorthaired pointer, Irish setter, Jack Russell terrier, Labrador retriever, malamute, Portuguese water dog, Rhodesian ridgeback, vizsla, wire fox terrier

Not surprisingly, pups in this personality category are extremely fit, with muscular bodies, lean frames, and no-nonsense coats that require little grooming. After all, a dip in the pool cures a bad hair day, right?

Some are larger dogs, others more on the short side, but all display that goofy, clownish yen for fun and games. Jocks are pretty low-maintenance dogs in the upkeep category, but they require extra attention in the physical-exercise bracket.

Jocks need to be played with daily, and they thrive in activities such as agility, fly ball, Frisbee, or canine freestyle. Some love to jog on the beach or swim laps in the pool. But all earn their varsity letters and are proud of them. One thing's for sure—owning a Jock is a sure way to get yourself to turn off the TV and go outside to play. Even if you don't have a kid who enjoys your love of sports or spending a Saturday tossing around the old pigskin, your Jock will fill that place. Gratefully.

Since Jocks are often found in a park or on the shoreline, they require names that are easy to shout and sound cool. This is not the place for a "Fluffernutter" or "Mr. Tink McStinkles." Jocks demand athletic-sounding names, strong monikers, and homages to famous athletes who share their love of the game. These no-frills names radiate respect and athleticism, both on and off the field.

Adonis—Lord

Amy—Beloved

Andre—Manly

Apollos—One who destroys

Archer—Athletic

Arlis—In charge

Armand—Strong soldier

Armstrong—One with a strong arm

Atalanta—Huntress

Audra—Noble strength

Austin—Great

Aviva—Renewal

Axel—My father is peace

Bacchus—Reveler

Beck—Brook

Beckett—Methodical

Becky—To tie

Billie—Determination, strength

Boone—Good

Bradac—Spirited

Brady—High-spirited

Brandon—High-spirited

Brent—Prepared

Brett—Innovative

Brice—Go-getter

Briscoe—Forceful

Brody—Builder

Brogan—Dependable

Brooke—Easygoing

Bryna—Strong one

Caine—Craftsman

Calhoun—Warrior

Callahan—Spiritual

Campbell—Bountiful

Carlin—Winner

Carly—Darling

Carter—Insightful

Cash—Conceited

Cayetano—Feisty

Ceres—Earth lover

Chaney—Strong

Chase—Hunter

Chaz—Manly

Chris—Bearer of Christ

Cody—Comforting

Cole—Lively, winner

Colt—Frisky

Connor—Brilliant

Conway—Brilliant

Corbin—Dark and brooding

Crawford—Flowing

Dakota—Friendly

Dale—Natural

Danica—Morning star

Dante—Enduring

Darian—Inventive

Dasha—Gift of God

Dave—Beloved

Dax—Unique

Deacon—Giving

Degan—Capable

Deion—Charismatic

Denley—Dark

Dericia—Athletic

Donovan—Combative

Doug—Strong

Drake—Dragonlike

Drew—Wise

Eitan—Strong

Elian—Spirited

Emma—Strong

Erla—Playful

Eunice—Winning

Eva—Life

Evander—Manly, champion

Faine—Happy

Faryl—Inspiring

Faxan—Outgoing

Fearghus—Strong man

Fia—Perky

Garvey—Rough

Grady—Noble

Graham—Warlike

Guy—Assertive, leader

Haim—Life

Hamon—Leader

Hawke—Watchful

Hunter—Adventurer

Iveta—Athletic

Ivy—Growing

Jack—God is gracious

CONTINUES ON PAGE 109

Heroic **NAMES**

Heroes come in all shapes, sizes . . . and species. Heroic dogs
have long been a part of our history. From saving lives to
serving as loyal companions, these notable canines have done
amazing things. What better way to honor their legacies than
name your puppy after one of them?

- **BALTO** was the lead sled dog on the final leg of the 1925 diptheria antitoxin serum run to Nome, Alaska. This heroic run was the inspiration for the Iditarod dog-sled race.

- **BARRY**, a Saint Bernard rescue dog, reportedly saved forty people.

- **BELKA** and **STRELKA** went into space aboard *Sputnik 5* and were the first to survive an orbital flight in 1960.

- **BOBBIE**, a collie-shepherd mix, traveled 2,800 miles home to Oregon after getting lost on a family trip to Indiana in 1923.

- **CINDY**, a greyhound, earned the *Guinness Book of World Record*'s Highest Jump by a Dog when she cleared a 5.5-foot hurdle.

- **GREYFRIARS BOBBY**, a loyal Skye terrier in Edinburgh, Scotland, spent fourteen years guarding his beloved master's grave, until he died in 1872.

- **GUINEFORT** became a saint in thirteenth-century England.

- **HACKIKO THE AKITA** used to wait for his owner after work at the train station—and he kept doing it daily for nine years after his owner's death.

- **HEIDI**, a Jack Russell terrier from Scotland, made her way down a 500-foot vertical drop to reach the body of her owner and stood guard over his body for days.

- **JIRO** and **TARO** survived after their dogsled team was left behind during a 1958 Japanese expedition to Antarctica. Their story inspired the film *Eight Below*.

- **LAIKA**, a Russian space dog, was launched into space on *Sputnik 2* and became the first being to orbit Earth in 1957. She died a few hours after launch from stress and overheating.

- **OLD SHEP**, a border collie, kept a vigil at a Montana train station, waiting for his master to return after seeing the coffin of his beloved owner loaded into a train in 1936. Old Shep was eventually killed by a passing train in 1942.

- **SERGEANT STUBBY** was the most decorated American war dog in World War I.

Jackson—Full of personality

Jade—Valued

Jagger—Brash

Jaime—Fun-loving

Jana—God is gracious

Janus—Optimistic

Jaren—Vocal

Jarrett—Confident

Jarvis—Athletic

Jason—Healer

Jenna—Sweet

Joel—The Lord is God

Johnny—God gave

Josh—Devout

Jules—Youthful

Juno—Queenly

Kai—Ocean

Kasey—Brave

Kate—Pure

Kizzie—Energetic

Klea—Bold

Knox—Bold

Kyle—Handsome

Lance—Confident

Lera—Strong

Leslie—Fiesty

Lois—Good

Luke—Worshipful

Maddie—Strength-giving

Marco—Warlike

Marylou—Athletic

Matt—Gift of God

Max—The greatest

McKenna—Able

Mia—Blessed

Mina—Strong-willed warrior

Monika—Adviser

Monya—Confident

Nash—Exciting

Nick— Victorious

Niko—Winning

Noel—Born on Christmas Day

Nolen—Renowned, noble

Ojas—Strong one

Parker—Keeper of the forest

Patrick—Nobleman

Paton—From the warrior's town

Pedro—Stone

Pete—Dependable

Peyton—From the fighter's farm

Pierce—Insightful

Porter—Keeper of the gate

Quinlan—Very strong

Ray—Counselor

Robin—Bright fame

Rocco—Tough

Rod—Brash

Rogan—Spirited redhead

Ron—Powerful, mighty

Ruby—A ruby jewel

Rudy—Famous wolf

Russell—Charmer

Ryan—Good-looking

Ryder—Outdoorsy

Scott—Happy

Scout—Observer

Serena—Serene, calm

Shane—God is gracious

Shannon—Wise one

Steve—Victorious

Tara—Towering

Tia—Princess

Tiergan—Strong-willed

Titus—Giant

Trevor—Wise

Troy—Good-looking

Tully—Powerful

Tyce—Lively

Tyee—Goal-oriented

Tyler—Industrious

Urban—From the city

Venus—Loving

Willa—Resolute guardian

Wyatt—Ready for combat

Wyn—Gregarious

Xylo—From the forest

Yael—Strength of God

Yaki—Tenacious

Zazula—Outstanding

MOST "pup-ular" DOG NAMES

If you want to go along with the pack, try one
of these tried-and-true names for your dog.

BOY DOG NAMES

Bailey	Oliver
Bandit	Oscar
Buddy	Riley
Casey	Rocky
Charlie	Rusty
Cody	Sam
Duke	Sammy
Gizmo	Samson
Harley	Shadow
Jack	Teddy
Jake	Toby
Lucky	Tucker
Max	Winston
Murphy	

GIRL DOG NAMES

Abby	Lady
Angel	Lucy
Annie	Maggie
Bailey	Missy
Bella	Misty
Brandy	Molly
Casey	Princess
Chloe	Rosie
Coco	Roxy
Daisy	Sadie
Emma	Samantha
Ginger	Sandy
Gracie	Sasha
Heidi	Sophie
Katie	Zoe

DIVA & THE PRETTY BOY

The Divas, and their Pretty Boy male counterparts, are a class unto themselves. These dogs believe we humans are here for their enjoyment. They adore looking their best, have a taste for the finest life has to offer, and refuse to entertain the notion that they are mere dogs.

Divas and Pretty Boys are delicately boned canines who often require daily grooming of their long or styled fur.

❧ MOST COMMON breeds ❧

affenpinscher, bichon frise, Chihuahua, Chinese crested dog, Lhasa apso, Maltese, papillon, Pekingese, Pomeranian, poodle, shar-pei, shih tzu, Yorkshire terrier

Some shake and get chills easily. Others have large eyes or an elegant, long-legged gait. The smaller-sized ones emit tinny, high-pitched barks. Many canines falling into this category are accustomed to being pampered beyond belief and actually expect it. They enjoy being on par with their owners, running errands with them, and being included in everything. Divas and Pretty Boys tend to be smaller dogs, as this lends itself best to the haute couture and designer dog carriers that tickle their fancy. Divas and Pretty Boys look at the world as if they only tolerate the craziness known as human existence. For they know best, and someday—sigh—we'll finally listen to them.

NAMES

Be it a beautiful name or a regal one, names for Divas and Pretty Boys must sound like music flowing off the tongue, and lend themselves to the sophistication, grace, and high-society air these dogs radiate. Some names can be influenced by popular culture (Paris Hilton, Naomi Campbell), while others are classics (Rhett Butler) that just ooze charm and grace. Even if the names' meanings don't exactly seem exotic or elegant, the way the names *sound* and the images they project embody what it truly means to be a Diva or a Pretty Boy.

Adora—Beloved one

Aiden—Little fire

Albert—Noble and bright

Alexis—Defender

Alistair—Defender of men

Anais—Gracious, merciful

Angelina—Messenger of God

Anthea—Lady of flowers

Anton—Highly praiseworthy

Antonetta—Praiseworthy

Antonia—Praiseworthy

Antony—Highly praiseworthy

Aoife—Beautiful, radiant

Arabella—Beautiful lion

Ash—Bold

Ashira—Wealthy

Ashton—Handsome

Augusta—Great

Aurora—Goddess of the dawn

Ava—Like a bird

Avery—Elf ruler

Ayanna—Beautiful blossom

Babette—My God is my oath

Basil—Regal

Basilius—Kingly

Beatrice—Bringer of joy

Bella—Beautiful

Belle—Beauty

Bellini—Little beautiful one

Bello—Handsome

Bianca—White, fair

Bijou—Jewel

Boaz—In strength

Braden—From the wide valley

Byron—Reclusive

Cadhla—Beautiful

Calix—Very handsome

Callia—Beautiful

Camilla—Perfect

Cassius—Vain

Cayden—Fighter

Celine—Heaven

Chandler—Ingenious

Channing—Knowing

Chauncy—Fortune

Christian—Follower of Christ

CONTINUES ON PAGE 118

Literary **NAMES**

Sure, your dog may never learn to read or write, but that doesn't mean you can't name her after your favorite author's pet or beloved literary character.

Argos—Odysseus's dog in Homer's *Odyssey*

Beautiful Joe—an abused Airedale rescued from a brutal master; he inspired an 1894 novel of the same name

Boatswain—the favorite pet of Lord Byron and the subject of his "Epitaph to a Dog"

Bounce—Alexander Pope's pet

Cerberus—the three-headed hound of Hades in Greek mythology

Charley—John Steinbeck's poodle, made famous by *Travels with Charley*

Clowder—from Shakespeare's *Taming of the Shrew*

Crab—from Shakespeare's *The Two Gentlemen of Verona*

Einstein—the dog in Dean Koontz's breakthrough novel *Watchers*

Fang—Hagrid's dog in the Harry Potter series

Flush—Elizabeth Barrett's cocker spaniel

Jacksie—a small dog belonging to C. S. Lewis

Lady and Tramp—from the Disney story *Lady and the Tramp*

Luath and Bodger—dogs in the book *The Incredible Journey*

Marley—the yellow Labrador retriever featured in John Grogan's memoir *Marley and Me*

Marlowe—Stephen King's Pembroke Welsh corgi

Nana—the Saint Bernard in *Peter Pan*

Old Dan and Little Ann—from *Where the Red Fern Grows*

Phiz—Helen Keller's dog

Pilot—Mr. Rochester's dog in *Jane Eyre*

Toto—from *The Wizard of Oz*

Tricki Woo—from *All Creatures Great and Small* by James Herriot

Trixie—Dean Koontz's beloved golden retriever, who "wrote" books before she died in 2007

Tyrant and Silver—from Shakespeare's *The Tempest*

Cleophas—Seeking glory

Crispin—Curly-haired

Damali—Beautiful vision

Darcy—Dark

Daria—Queenly

Daylin—Beautiful day

Delphine—Calmness

Dermott—Free man

Desiree—Desired

Dimitri—Goddess of the harvest

Diva—Divine one

Eavan—Beautiful radiance

Edmund—Rich protector

Elias—Jehovah is God

Emlen—Charming

Esme—Kind defender

Evangeline—Like an angel

Fayre—Beautiful

Feodora—God-given girl

Finlay—Fair warrior

Fiona—Fair-haired

Fleur—Flower

Franchesca—Free

Francis—Free

Frederick—Peace ruler

Gabriella—God is my strength

Gareth—Gentle

Giselle—Devoted friend

Hasana—Beautiful, fair

Hiraani—Beautiful sky

Ian—God is gracious

Ileannah—Soaring

Indah—Beautiful one

Ione—Violet flower

Irene—Peace

Isabella—God is my oath

Isolde—Beautiful

Jasmine—Jasmine

Jayden—Bright-eyed

Jolie—Pretty

Jules—Youthful

Julia—Downy, soft

Julian—Gorgeous

Juliana—Youthful

Keegan— Ball of fire

Kenzie—Handsome

Kiara—Bright

Leland—Protective

Leonardo—Bold lion

Leopold—Bold

Letitia—Joy

Lola—Pensive

Lorelei—Siren

Lorelle—Lovely

Loren—Picture-perfect

Lucinda—Light

Madonna—My lady

Malcolm—Follower of Saint Columbus

Marcella—Young warrior

Marius—Virile

Mercedes—Merciful

Merrick—Ruler of the sea

Mirabel—Of uncommon beauty

Misha—Who is like God

Monique—Adviser

Naomi—Beautiful, gentle

Natasha—Born on Christmas Day

Nevaeh—Heaven

Odelia—I will praise God

Olympia—From Olympus

Orman—Noble

Paloma—Dove

Pandora—All gifts

Paris—From Paris

Percival—Mysterious

Percy—Piercing the valley

Petra—Stone, rock

Philippa—Lover of horses

Phineas—Farsighted

Portia—A giving woman

Priscilla—Wisdom of the ages

Quentin—Fifth

Reid—Redheaded

Rhett—Counsel, advice

Rhys—Loving

Rian—Little king

Rupin—Handsome

THE DIVA & THE PRETTY BOY

Sabrina—From the River Severn

Saffron—Yellow flower

Salome—Peace

Sasha—Defending men

Scarlett—Red

Sebastian—Venerable

Selena—Like the moon

Simon—One who hears

Sinead—Believer in a gracious God

Siobhan—Believer, lovely

Sohan—Charming

Sophia—Wisdom

Suzette—Lily

Tania—Fairy queen

Tatiana—Fairy queen

Teodora—God's gift

Tiara—Crowned goddess

Trina—Perfect

Tristan— Impulsive

Umika—Goddess

Urania—Heavenly

Uri—My light

Valentina—Strength, health

Venetia—Woman of Venice

Violet—Purple flower

Wesley—Bland

Weston—Good neighbor

Xander—Defender of men

Yancy—Vivacious

Yvette—Lively archer

Zain—Handsome

Zara—Princess

VACCINES 101

Vaccines are a part of a healthy puppy's life. Yet despite their necessity, they can be a confusing part of dog ownership. Talk with your veterinarian and educate yourself about the basics of canine vaccinations. Remember, these guidelines should be considered secondary to your veterinarian's recommendations as well as your dog's individual needs, health issues, and living conditions.

Puppies first receive their shots at six to nine weeks, guarding against diseases like adenovirus, distemper, and parvovirus (see list), with boosters around sixteen weeks. Rabies vaccines usually occur at the end of the vaccination series. Every state is different and has its own requirements about this vaccine, so check with your veterinarian. Keep your puppy away from strange dogs and popular hangouts (like parks) until initial vaccines are complete. Ask your veterinarian for permission before exposing your dog to these things.

YOUR PUPPY WILL MOST LIKELY RECEIVE VACCINATIONS PROTECTING AGAINST DISEASES SUCH AS:

- **CANINE DISTEMPER**—causes coldlike symptoms, vomiting, diarrhea, fever, and convulsions. More than half of affected dogs and three-quarters of affected puppies die. Survivors face permanent damage to the nervous system. There is no cure, but treatment helps ease the symptoms.

- **CANINE PARVOVIRUS**—causes bloody diarrhea, vomiting, fever, loss of appetite, and depression. Sometimes mistaken for "doggie flu." Usually fatal to puppies, especially without immediate treatment. Rottweilers, Doberman pinschers, and other black and tan breeds are especially prone to this disease. There is no cure, but antibiotics and IV fluids are used to manage symptoms.

- **CANINE ADENOVIRUS-1 (CAV-1)**—causes severe liver disease, nausea, vomiting, loss of appetite, jaundice, light-colored stool, and stomach enlargement. Prognosis ranges from very good to sometimes fatal.

- **CANINE ADENOVIRUS-2 (CAV-2)**—a highly contagious but rare virus causing upper respiratory infections and a dry, hacking cough. Vaccine also protects against CAV-1. Prognosis ranges from poor to good, depending on the dog's condition and age.

- **RABIES**—a fatal virus that affects the brain and spinal cord. Symptoms include vague to severe changes in temperament, restlessness, nervousness, viciousness, gnawing angrily on themselves, frothing at the mouth, and bloody saliva. There is no known cure or treatment.

- **BORDETELLA**—common "kennel cough." Treatment usually focuses on symptoms; occasionally antibiotics are needed.

- **BORRELIA BURGDORFERI (LYME DISEASE)**—caused by ticks. Fever, lethargy, swelling in the bitten limb, joint pain, lameness, and depression. Treatable with antibiotics. Occasionally can have chronic effects, especially on joints.

ACKNOWLEDGMENTS

Special thanks to the folks at becker&mayer!, especially editors Amy Wideman and Meghan Cleary, for giving me this opportunity. I'm also grateful for the help of James J. Watson, D.V.M., of the Villa Park Animal Clinic for his information. Thanks to the folks at *Dog Fancy* magazine for starting me on this wonderful road of dog writing. Thanks, Mom and Dad, for being so proud of my writing, giving me such a unique name, and inspiring my lifelong love of names and books. I'll always be grateful. To my amazing daughter, Kieran, for making me a better person and teaching me the true meaning of joy. To my husband and fellow dog lover, Patrick—thank you for all the support and encouragement. And to my wonderful dogs, Annie and Owen, who changed my life, prepared me for parenthood, and make me happy every day. You will always be a part of me.

KYRA KIRKWOOD is a professional writer and lifelong dog lover. Since graduating from the University of Southern California's School of Journalism in 1993, she has worked as a journalist for numerous magazines, newspapers, and other publications, covering everything from city government to movie premiers. But her true calling came when she began writing articles for *Dog Fancy* magazine as well as dog-themed columns in Los Angeles–area newspapers. Since then, dog reporting has taken top billing. Kyra focuses much of her journalism work on helping ease the plight of homeless and abused dogs. She adopted her two dogs, Annie and Owen, from animal shelters, and she also volunteers with various dog rescue groups. When she's not writing about or helping dogs, Kyra enjoys yoga, photography, traveling, and spending time with her husband and daughter. More about Kyra can be found at www.KyraKirkwood.com.

INDEX